IN A FUGITIVE SEASON

In A Fugitive Season

A Sequence of Poems

Robert Dana

THE SWALLOW PRESS
THE OHIO UNIVERSITY PRESS
ATHENS, OHIO

CHICAGO

LONDON

Published by
The Ohio University Press
1980

Originally published in 1979 (Ltd. Ed.) by
The Windhover Press
University of Iowa
Iowa City, Iowa

ISBN (cloth edition) 0-8040-0804-3
ISBN (paper edition) 0-8040-0805-1

Library of Congress Catalog Card Number 80-7783

This book is for my children:
Lori, Arden, and Richard

and for Peg

I ❧ *So, what if reality may be terrible?*
It's better than what we've got.

Saul Bellow

A man is only as good as what he loves.

Saul Bellow

1 ● Flatnosed Chinese Sappho
I love you

If I say
the sky runs to a blue glaze
in the bottom of my dish

or
the moon is the sweetness of long bones

will you believe me?

2 ● I remember the day began
a giant flag whacking the air
two Japanese boys fishing in the Field Museum

Mrs. Marvellous bores me
She knows her stuff
She has the proper enthusiasm
But I am pushing packmules through snow
a scarred head about to speak
a wooden Buddha without hands

Farther north in a room of smoke
Inouye-san calls down his own Buddha into the June heat
It shouts from the next porch
in the southern mountain voice of a boy
'Allright then.
If you do that,
you love Alice Miller Period No Changes.'

The fire dies
The windows have been opened and there is tea
At the bottom of the glass
from under ice strong lemon cleans the mouth

Behind me
I leave shadow on the ground

3 ● That morning
is only as you remember it
imperfectly

[And

And a woman
walks the green mall lightly
in her own light summer dress

She is neither the woman
who started toward you
nor she who will finally arrive

At your window
the first white insects of winter
sting the glass

4 ❧ In flat-bottomed grey planes
in domes   in lofts of swollen cumulus
the sky slides into this slicked blacktop
into puddles along the road

And I am driving into my own sleep
of white chickens
Past barnyard harvests of junked cars
The wind slumping through the eyes of cows

What holds me now arcs like a speedometer
is marked like my own hand
As if behind my face was a life I couldn't help
Three lives I hadn't enough love for

5 ❦ The Prisoners

They lie under claws of light
who have been sentenced to their own names
all their lives

Day after day after day after day passes
and they do not change
The laughter of turnkeys flashes its teeth

Their nights try them
and they find no moment when it didn't happen
Their memories fume odorless as gas

In these apartments
where they had not hoped to live
they dream with their eyes open

6 ● Night is falling on Williamsport
All day
out of this valley of the Susquehanna
water has been rising toward the sun

Our business has prospered in a heavy fur
our breath had the odor of mines
we are no longer sure what we should ask for

Across the glass of this elaborate house
an airliner cruises like a dish of zircons

This side of the picture the frame is straight
dinner smokes on the table
the children are waiting

On the wall two peaches ripen in empty space
Behind them
the rice-sparrows the mountain we have been told we cannot see

We take each other's hands
We sit silently in the blind distance

7 ● She is not herself
There is nothing she has not wanted

but the room has kept to its own whiteness

She has seen the sky gather on the river
seen it skid over the falls into a flock of water
Wind slid over her arm like warm nylon

Knowing that yes is a question she'd loved him
She did not need
to be able to say so

But waking into this room
her breath itches
with something he left no trace of

Should she consult her marvellous shoes
they would tell her nothing
five floors above the ground

Let her walk down to the morning fire-haired

[trailing

trailing her darkness behind her into the wet grass
Let her enter the schoolroom of broken children

She will teach them to touch their anger with the tips of their fingers

8 ● Morning blows from the northwest

Around her elms are dying
Teeth shriek in their carcasses
All day they will fall for burning

Her heart beats in her ears
Her breath is wet silver
She walks the weeds barefoot speaking their names to the water

Buckhorn   Lambsquarters   Sheep-Sorrel
Yellow Rocket   Black Medic   Heal-All

Fish tug the sun into silent targets on the lake

It's all there
the emptiness gentle in her hands

9 ● Elsewhere
the others have fallen into silence
Their shoes mumble of Fun City
Sleep seizes the elevators

And all night
tanks vanish into the eyes of infantry
The rain tastes of smoke
The dead desert him in arbors of wire

In the camps
what are the children singing of
where are the old men
Everywhere the eyes of the women are empty
Everywhere ignorance occurs perfectly in the flags of the State

Now
his room speaks its black syllable
Time is luminous at his wrist
He dreams he's Inspector of Snowstorms
that he's been trying to live
that he almost begins

10 ● We listened for it at the wind's back
that darkness you can hear

It slips down
under trees leaved with fire
as if to the river's edge
sipping the waters like some familiar animal

In the bright vowels of three puddles
it remembers bare stone

Now it seems important to ignore ourselves
to undress into our own flesh
to gather from the earth its sharp fires

It seems important
to make no move the snow will look back on

11 ● In Memoriam, RFK

It's been evening all day
Midwinter rain sleek and raw

Nine days it's been falling on L. A.
Great trees gutter
Canyons with their houses slump into the sea

Now trucks are made ready again
and refugees shake the darkness from their shoes
They hear grief hum in the heavy metal

Some are relieved to be carrying away nothing
Some bear letters of introduction
Some knives

The trucks move out in the direction of the mountains
None asks where

At first light
small birds cry in Syrian
and the wolf lies on the left side of his blood
slowing into sleep

12 ● Nothing sharpened his days
The winter and the snow
                                                        [the

the snow in successive ripples successive waves
cresting into scarps by the roadside wire
The winter and the snow
The sun on the snow in the broken encampments of stalks
His fields burning like white phosphorous

Nothing sharpened his days
He was nothing he'd imagined
nights the fire kneeled into itself in the darkened room
Where was she now the bitch of his salts and oils
It surprised him in the act of completeness
that the body is god's fool the fool his library
The winter and the snow

Nothing
A season of minimums
Beyond the end-table
where her nameless houseplant flourished in a clay vase
they clung even to spring in patches scattered like forty years
the winter and the snow

13 ● At the Bureau of Machines
    morning sleeps in the eyes

    I check my cards for credit and I. D.
    I exist
    The lines on my hands are criminal

    Answers are the condolence of questions
    the profits of loss

    Now
    things have returned to their places
    Blocks of actuaries
    Avenues of secretaries from their hopes

    The shop windows are dressed in fantasies of importance
    Wires twitch
    Hands change pockets

    In all of this the craftsman does not leave his mark

    In the lesser precincts
    the poor have made of their disgrace a magical secret

They are filming the official movie of desire
Even the white actors are black
and the script they do not have has been rehearsed
'Death is the only real elegance'

Somewhere my father the fabulous milliner is opening his doors

14 ❧ Across the lake the capitol swelters
Power sleeps in its brass crib
like a beautiful child with nothing in her sleeves

The guardsmen have left
taking with them the order of knives
The legislators have closed their teeth on the law and gone home

In the streets of the city
the young make a carnival in their clothes
They say 'We have died too often'
They say 'We have not lived'

We are what has become of them

We sit here
It is night still to the bottom of the sky
Somewhere beyond our vision a boat is moving
Its waves argue with the soft beach

We have believed too little

I am the angler at the edge of darkness
You are morning in the orange garden of your dress

Here is the savage   the simple
Blind worth

    man   woman   water returning   earth

15 ❧ A boredom of summer storms
something about her of the sun resents

The trying to be real
The narrow act

At night the zag zag zag of sodium lamps

                                                    [blue

blue across the causeways
Rain running the gravure of Suburbia-on-the-Water

The lake tells the terrible story of light
Once wild with the near woods
it ached of its clear festivity

And she wants the taste of that life
That twitter of sparrows on a spinal wire
That coming free

But she eats her own perfect hunger

And afterwards   the dishes   the cats
the unreadable book of her own persuasion

She sleeps naked and alone
troubling the sheets
The moon behind its storm-clouds vanishing into glass

16 ❧ We lose the houses barging up the river
the egrets among the islands   the islands

The river runs away into the narrows
We lose the day in the white rain

You remember a stone heavy as a gift
Your mouth tastes like bread

I remember a little girl saying
'Death means somebody has to kiss you'

We have driven into the radio's excuses
into the touch at the end of our headlights

Without names the tall rocks pass us
soaked in our slow live breathing

II   ❷   *Come, your answer in broken music . . .*

Good is what we can do with evil.

Begin with the lies of sun and moon
day and night sitting at the same table
the eye of fire and the eye of glass

Their light lies upon the sea in colors
Upon the luffed sails
or sensible on the deep backs of its creatures

At bottom   darkness
great jaws hurrying behind their own lights
through cold tons of pressure

The sea fumes
The clouds are thin or heavy
shifting and busy in the lie of the wind

We are foolish
We believe in their possibilities
in rain

in the odor of lightning in electric meadows
in the laughter of trees
appearances   small vanishings   renewals

in the charities of bone and pollen
the small lies of the cricket and the wren
in the framing of houses

Lying is nature we say
and lying well is an art
and as both have it another way we say

There are lies like an empty glove
like lover's fingers
like a rich woman stealing butter

dime-store lies
the nifty pocket-knives of our own advice
the watchman's footfall in the empty yard

Lies like the machines of our miracle with no moving parts
like cards with holes in them for nothing
like celebrations intricate with fire and air

I'll settle for all of them
                                                    [settling

settling for a world that comes apart like a surprise
and all is imaginable

For the voice in the next room useless and reasonable
as the sea is delicate and muscular
running under such dreams as run under our lives

18 ◐ He'd asked too much of the day
not to be troubled

of his body both as wheel and burden
of his own anguished magic

that no memory of her should rise from the lucky grass

There being only one of anything
that he should lose his touch for the little
the sanity that makes eyes beautiful

But the wind rolls from one of its lesser sleeps
the sun shakes the pond
the bones of his vision flutter up like birds
and spring
makes of itself the first loneliness of touching her

Last month in Atlanta
the southern hush of money like the strum in a cat's throat
and cardinals popping in wooded suburbs
And before that
a range of western mountains
falling away in white-capped blue combers to the north

These made of themselves whatever uselessness was necessary

Now he whistles under the true sky of his troubles
walking slowly
inside himself

Tell him you see him thus
Give him the names of her inconsistencies
There being only one of anything
tell him the past will not get better

19 ◐ The small towns of the strange middle of our lives
remain small

Streets
wintry even in summer

Here the old forget themselves
in their own stories
the moon rises
the town's tower lifts its silver planet of water into the sky
and the children believe in God
and the cold gardens of his weather

What makes of such poor wisdom
the knife of the will
of such poverty
the flower without memory
we do not know

Tonight
men wire their bodies to grenades
jets sizzle blind from the decks of carriers
In the streets
something dies

If our heads flamed here once
If together we rolled
and the sun rolled
like a pride of lions through the summer grass
and our teeth clicked with a fever
it was another world

where the day was called by your name and mine
and love was another name for sight

Now the cat stirs beside me
in the deep hair of its sleep
and my envy stirs
that last of my rights
even that frail mania

Too far arrived to go back
I see that I am what I always was

that ordinary man on his front steps
bewildered under the bright mess of the heavens
by the fierce indecipherable language of its stars

for Mary

No sweetness so heavy
as the beef and muggy heft of summer

The sun lays down in the fields at the edge of town
its broken sentence of black cattle

No hunger so full of teeth for sugar as the addict's
Shining into the bruised vein

The light of every object
in its terrible necessity
scattering dead on its edges

Only the truly useless is beautiful

His blood stutters
His gaze stutters to its own dark center
Any month steps in the breath of foul clothes
and kisses his fear

No taste so sure for the shining water
for the deep juice of cherries
as the woman's

in whose husband's hands
the past is satisfied

But there is a voice in the voices of her children
rain over rain
and the beach working in her silence
that makes her turn
and touch the hot spatter of pinks
in a milk-glass bowl

What we crave
is what we have

light for the long season
this table wooden as the loneliness of plain fact
this cup of cold tea

And bread for the moon
the heart's small loaf

21 ❧ Things are as they were

Another season gone
Another summer deepened and grown heavy

Each day the sun
the white fires of cloud
the inexhaustible heat
Haze walling the distances

The air off the fields is enormous

Nothing is left of that other morning
its colors
its whistle
its water embers

'I have this passion' she says 'to sit out the next ten years'
'I have the wise woman's spite'
'I'm not his mother or his mistress or his wife'

A damsel-fly hovers
A blue sliver of direction

The trees   the houses   the sky
shine up inverted
from the surface of the lake

Returning alone
to this familiar place
what had she hoped to find
so perfect to lose

22 ❧ Grey day after day
cold
and the rain moving toward him again

If he sleeps
it's like a burning building
If he dreams
it's of neither fire nor water

        •

This is love's blind corner
This is shadow

                                    [In the

In the moonlight
the slick ponies carouse and are riderless

Where dogs take the darkness in their teeth
lover's take their silence in their arms
and night turns
in the complexity of its disasters

But theirs are no more than they have made them
Nothing is simple

Between them
loneliness is what's left of the sacred
In the inner kiss of breath
the marriage
the laughter

         ❧

When he wakes
the meadows of this dream are empty

23 ❧ The day falls from its brilliant skin
He knows where it goes
'It's a sad successful story'

Another month
and the pond struck blind with December ice
will give back no remembrance

Not of her naked feet
Not of the smoking faces of horses
Not of the clouds swelling
Nor the waters nippling and swelling
the trees releasing everywhere their dry fires

And having become strange to his own body
he will touch his hands
and something will stand up in his blood
and walk forth
wearing only the thin shirt of his nerves

Where she is
the seasons blur and that is mercy
The flavor of dust in the grapes has a Spanish name
she lolls on her tongue

when the wind totters
and the windows turn to water

Of all that she has forgotten
she has made for herself a serious life
So says the garden
So say the lissom steams of her kitchen
So says the fire-shape asleep by the door

'Give thyself
And keeping whole thou shalt prosper'

They have rejected what was easy
Out of deep
sudden spaces risen up to be husbanded or wived
or cornered into disparate seasons
Out of pity or love or anger

But who can compute the angles of angels
or complete this blue dusk
this flaring blue teeter of water
where the sun sinks like a breath torn whole out of heaven

Here is the beginning of the beginning
they would begin again

24 ❧ Chicago, Midwinter

The city rises below them
like cakes of pure ice

or spills away like a shatter of jewels

If the iron ape hunches in the plaza
In the cold
if the manhunt is on

still from the great lake
the surf loops steadily toward the shore

blessing them with its indifference

They will not lose tomorrow
nor the silver key in the ashtray
nor the sense of the door closing behind them

[Though

Though they will not find
the perfect rings they looked for

In the winter park
it will not seem strange to them
that their madness warms
and casts its light across the snow

25   *Passover*

Monday is the moon
A supper of ovum and blood yolk
madness in a dark mouth

Tuesday is two days
A cloud of spiders drifts over Corpus Christi toward the Gulf
where if touch is truth
your skin is a listener

Dressed in Wednesday black
a white-faced ex wife
keeps his voice low for his daughters his lost son
Her hands are the kitchens of suicide
They will not cease

Thursday is itself all day
The morning paper campaigns in the hall
What will the next president preside over of purpose
In news resembling this
it snows
It will not be spring

And if he once concedes
how nothing of necessity passes into the face of its kind
Friday will be Passover
will be wine
a meal of horseradish and bone
they will be lucky they need not eat

To Saturday
he returns the long book that reads
'To see is to be lonely'
'Beauty is the beginning of a terror we're just able to endure'

And Sunday he stands
at all eleven doors of the five rooms of his life
The windows bubble with wet light
The floors have been washed
old furnishings brushed and polished

26 ❧ Once more
the eye of the pond blinks open

The lap of waters
Bright webs
birches spin of themselves from moonlight

Amnios
Amnios
a whole imagined country
waking in that wild radiance that shakes my life

And knowing only that name
by which I may speak of her
I try to dream in her language
whatever realities of touch touch in her

Put on the face of another
and you will see with new eyes
Put on the skin of another
and you will sweat in his personal darkness
Take upon your tongue the words of another
and you will hear them
and yourself in them

I am turmoil
come here like pride
the bite of little sour apples on its tongue

I am pleasure
come here like pain walking deep
I dazzle and freeze
I spin and burn
deep into the marrow of my life

I am Gandhi and salt and the serene wheel
And tonight
an empire of needs is collapsing in all this silver

Deep in its throat
the mountain holds its breath

Silence has its rights

Gradual as sleep
the heat rises
the footpath rises in the red earth

Bells of white yucca
Up sheer stone
pines flying on their great dark wings

If we could
in our breathing
we would touch everything everywhere at once
But we are not the reason
nothing here needs us

Even this stone
lifted from its triangular shining
Even this tree
dry instrument broken to weather
to one commanding branch

These are holiness slipped from its first shapes
They keep their distances

Slick over the rocks
the water falls
and we give our faces to it
and take its cold on our tongues
and into our calm bodies its silver quaking

It is July
It is early evening

Darkness swarms on the water

and on this hunch of rock
where we have eaten
the wind speaks to us from the mouths of bottles

I see the mountains
roll up beneath themselves

In the cool and perfect sunlight
the clear anniversaries of distance

I'm aware
that you're not here   not wholly
Aware of half the silence in your words

The late afternoon
takes us up into a kingdom of swallows
They veer and plunge
Commanding our breath

A man may come a long way to hear bad news

may look into the light
steadily and for a long time
and still see nothing

As if he'd taken the sky into his side

Frightened
and a little strange to myself

as if I'd wakened on the couch
something without a name

I sit down beside your absence
I sit by your breath

and draw my best arguments about me
against the empty chairs

I ask myself

'If I close my eyes
will my hands still be wise for you'

The soul remembers in the sense

That pale cloud coasting your arm
the dipper of brown stars between your shoulders
The imaginable bones under your face

I ask myself

'What time is it by the white daisies in the field'

30 ● Trees and two green lakes
the sun's expectant and hushy engines

Also the road
clenched into itself like a muddy nerve

These I have without you

Sunlight
wet with the fire of a drunken spider
bobs on a thread

And outside another window
the reflection of the next
hangs its empty mirror on the air

31 ◗ Sunlight off the snow

snow frozen and thawed and frozen again
to this silver mesh

The road is like iron meal
where his boots feed

He is walking out on his ambitions
sloughing the burning sleep of his vanity
the silence of power in the face of need

Having made the mistakes
others give their names to
he keeps that danger in his pocket and the wind close

He follows the tangled winter edge of some nerve in his head

under the high pines
past the lake
its still open water shining and black as a collapsed star
into the distance where the crow barks its warning

Where whatever is true
everything falls that must rise

32 ◗ The Gift of Fire

Christmas day
and the pines misted above the heavy snow

A bird ghosts the far clearing

All of this sleeps in the President's head

His radar whispers
and universities fall out of the sky
the rot of cities
the milk of poverty in your letters saying 'I love you'
and 'I still love you but goodbye'
fall toward their targets

When the black kiss explodes
and gut ribbons out in the unbelievable decompression
or the heart ruptures in those silver altitudes

it is not more
than the scream in the streets
when the gift of fire opens itself

How then shall the child be known
the carpenter bleeding into the beatiful grain of his labor
the mother her breasts blown away
How then shall the ash of the grandfathers be honored

As I walk the wheel-rutted snow
following my own tracks of the day before
and those of the dog and a man on bear-paws

I come to your name
where I knifed it into the snow
and I try to shape one word I can believe

33 ❧ It was not quite winter
when we first walked here

The blue air dripped and spattered
the flags of the lookout sweated cold

damp limestone upon stone

Across the river
the trees had banked their wet fires
'God moves in the wind' you said 'if he moves at all'

Today
in this not quite spring

[the

the wind full
the sun like silver birds
flocking the water with its passion

we hunker
against the south sides of stones

warm and animal

34 ● Love's Body

Woman beside me
your hair about my wrist is a rope of honey

And when you touch me with your eyes
with the flower of your mouth
our nakedness makes of itself the naked truth

Marriage is the flesh of our deep delight

I am your own lean animal
the bear sucking the warm fruit of your breasts
the fox at your belly
the hound at your hip
high on the sweet scents of your marrow

Ah wife
stroke the fur of my breath in your lap

As I press my lips to that witches' moss of stiff curl
and kiss your legs with my tongue
tip forth your salts
your delicate ciders
the tenderest silver of the tastes of your body

Pleasure glows at all your proud openings
as you take me into yourself
as you lift yourself toward me like wonder

35 ● Vision and Transformation

Of his right hand
he has made for her
the five roots of the tree of his arm
Of its strength

the twist and reach of branches
and some deep scent remembered of the earth

where her wish is a wing
the feather of small birds in the leaves
safe when the dusk comes down

Of his left hand
he has made for her the five lean bones of hunger
a dog of knuckle and gristle
rough furred
and of a silver cunning

She touches him
He becomes legend and sleeps beside her

He has made for her a house of his body
A kiss of wind in the eaves
Night drops from its windows like raw silk

On a table
a bowl of oranges
the glow of clear water
the coarse black bread of his longing

Where she moves
the breath of her work sings
and morning lengthens into the flavor of grace

36 ❧ The Watergate Elegy

Justice corrupts

All those years of spying
years of fear
The cold tit of the Capitol

No man can afford to lose his best enemies

The White House white as cake
there must have been months
when whole Mafias of black limousine kissed the curb
drab captains debouching with report
lieutenants packing heavy info

[And

And out of New Jersey through Mexico
Out of the Florida Keys
Out of San Clemente to Angel City
what couriers ferrying tropical memoranda
what sugars carried for silence

The politic is power
suspicion the currency of its hunger
lies property to be kept safe under combinations

Sicken waters
Die land
And if the citizen eat his rights for bread and meat
in such least light
the kept counsels prosper

Spring is long gone from this city
The mallards
shackled to their Potomac slough in a surprise of ice
waiting for the sun to warm
They too are gone

This city is not a wheel for nothing
not white for nothing amid its blacks and cherry trees

But the axle is broken
the hub empty

And at the end of his reflection
Lincoln shrinks into the dark memorial of his penny

37 ❧ Valentine

your back is a white heart
my prick a stiff flower

I brush your hair
In this dry darkness its sparks fly

Your nipples lift
Your wet bones open their own dark

where every evening
takes its blue beginning

In my hands
I feel the warm moons of your ass rising

'make no travel preparations
until you arrive'

Tiny stars of seed
shower

extinguish in the night-room

Woman
fucking you is a race through a long black train

We are two separate leaps of blood

We kiss for breath

38 ❦ *In Memoriam*, M S H, *1929-1974*

Lady Moon
Thin dime

fair to what lost day

girlhood lost in the toilet bowl
the blood dark and gorgeous
in those cramped curls

Behind you
did Minnesota's fields grow green

your voice
pour its silver lieder on a summer air

Did the nights groan
fat with men and babies

In the end
in the bad movie of your mind

was it only February again
morning again

the stuck gear chattering
the image clouding

doldrums of snow straying those northern roads
on a huge and bitter wind
                  [the

the scream inside you
cold cash

O sweet Christ   O
crazy sermon on the speed of light

39 ● The need to die
is the need

to change color and religion
politics

to change planetary relations
the need to change positions

Others have known it
and screamed

We speak
or keep silent

The laughter of your coming
shakes at the end of you

where I lie down for love
amid the weapons of your bones

40 ● Bittersweet Ode

Grey breath of a day
The whip of briars

Smiling and tired
you lie here on the matted grass

burst embers
of cut bittersweet

glowing rich
and orange

And beneath you
the careless darkness of roots

the chilled black dirt
where your sisters the two crickets are singing

41 ● In the house of friends
in a cold room

I read
and my eyes burn

A pressure of blood
shifts itself under my cheekbones

Fatigue
has wintered in my clothes all day

And all day
the schoolchildren have said

'We don't care'
'Energy is death Pal'

A cough in our engines
A kick in the head

Nobody's cat
mangled to meat and hair

bloody
on the highway stripe

'But death is breath
Kid' I say

Live space
leaps between our bones

Warm bramble
of stars

Venice
rising from a snowy sea

Kid this planet
does its crazy slow turn under us

And miles away
even my midwestern burg

twinkles
through the blue drizzle

III   ☻   *France was a land, England was a people, but America, ...*
was harder to utter. . . . It was a willingness of the heart.

F. Scott Fitzgerald, 1929

. . . Let me have
the courage to live
as fictions live, proud, careless
unwilling to die . . . .

Philip Levine, 1965

42 ✿ Snow
And St. Mary's tolling Christmas over the stricken fields

the good friends
scattered and silent

❧

We have grown thin
on the gossip of others

Their
green salads

Their talk
of desserts

❧

Dine this season
only with strangers

Or your wife
and children

On red apples   peaches
cold sweet pears

43 ❧ '...hurry hurry hurry hurry hurry...'
ticks into this English cold

The clock's face stupid
amid golden cupidons

And in its ring of brushed silver
The black Imperial numbers

❧

The color of the cold
is the color of the sun

Pieces of sky
fall through the mail slot

and your voice comes to me as long late-afternoon shadows
across the garden saying

'This is the house'
'This is the door'

❧

[If

If I reply
I reply   'Between Thou
                    and Thou'

Am I the Marx or the Lenin of husbands
And what papers shall I leave for the Revolution

44 ✸ The morning goes by under water

He thinks of his young wife
of her face and body   her voice

On the long dining table
two journals

the red portable
with its lettered fingernails

a packet of fresh envelopes
their edges slashed red and blue

Under the address book
the calendar shows March

the days crossed out through 10

And under these
the notes for a poem

'Hot-dogs by the lake

Water and sky by Whistler
A regatta of angels'

The rest is a scattering of slips   mixed business
A cartridge of spent film

At 5 the sun comes out

the biography of a clean plate
the biography of two Moroccan oranges and a knife

The morning goes by under water

He thinks of his friend who wears a bloodstone
He thinks of his wife

    for Phil and Peg

45 ❧ Hostages

The end of April
Suetonius Paulinus

Blossoming
And still after rain you can see your breath

You must have frozen
your Roman balls off here

And here I am
camped at this fag end of two empires

near walls you built to imprison hostages
hostage to myself

In the square
tulips rich as a clutch of Easter eggs

Chilled bees
sway across the grass

And no one speaks your language
gristle of twenty legions

or for that matter Suetonius Paulinus
mine

46 ❧ Hawks, Snow, and Plum
(after a screen by Nichokan Soga)

On matched silk
the gold sky bends away before them

empty
but for three white clouds

Crusted with snow
two trunks of plum twist leafless from the rock

And the hawks
one poised to fly   the other in fierce repose

remain there
among the blood-bright flowers

On an afternoon
suffused with just such light

[we

we have been here
somewhere else

You are tall
with lovely moves under your clothes

And I listen to you
listen

Where stone
suggests This house This snow

And amid green leaves
the tulip tree lifts its extravagant bloom

47 ❧ *Elegy for the Duke*

Ellington is dead

A-train down from Harlem
Tiger-jawed dashikis flashing down from Harlem

Plum and burgundy and fire

Here
London plays a low-tide blues

spice of tar
gulls over brown water

And at the Tate
Turner dissolves us all into pure light

into Eleanor Rose and Argonaut and Thames Brittania

Weather as soul

The world turning over

48 ❧ Sweet Williams for you
Billy Blake

set down before your fire-blackened gravestone
by my wife

her rust blouse new
and freckled with cherries

In this 'green and pleasant land'
Jerusalem rots

And south of the old leper hospital
your truths

are still chalked
in the streets

'Tip Everest is King'
'J loves K'

49 ☙ *Driving North Wales*

Off Anglesey
the sea is blue and calm

Beaumaris
where the curious walk in ruins

Herring gulls
A nose-diving plastic kite

Up the coast
we stop for tea

A pack of daws
wigged and black-beaked

flutters from the sea-wall
Thieves and judges

In the late afternoon
rare sunlight

the water curls and flashes
Crouched before it

looking out toward ruined Ireland
listening to the English end their sentences with questions

I hunt the shallows
for flat smooth stones

Behind me
the mountains fly their rags of cloud

and in Welsh meadows
the cattle kneel down to promise rain

for Ken and Elsie Lawson

You are dying on Madeira

Below your beach-chair
the sea natters

We are all far away

Or is it evening there
the moon pouring down its strange light

You adjust your tie
as you wade in

Your pants fill
with the cold weight of water

Laughing at yourself
you cannot stop weeping

Nothing flows into your eyes

In your room
the slack tongues of soiled clothing

speak from the mouth of the dresser

Letters unfinished
unmailed

say '. . . this lovely island . . .'
'I don't see anything ahead'

This is your room

because it's white
and its windows overlook the sea

Your room
and unacceptable

51 ☙ Nothing but eyes
nothing but bone and tongue

Sprawled survivors
to strip under these prehistoric clouds

Seed
and the light in the grass

flash between your legs
here on this dead man's barrow

and for days
I'll carry your smell on my hands like the sea

Behind us
Stonehenge wrecks

Its heelstone
lunging toward mid-summer

In my own country
in another season

I'll kneel before ashes
kindling their fire with my breath

In the evening of each ear
you'll wear

small beads of blood
looped on golden wires

Envoi

Down country
Missouri still dreams of plantations

July scorches
to Independence and the weather

By dusk
all the pie has been eaten

flies sleep on the ceilings of heavy verandas
the day slows and softens

Spear by spear
grasses burnt blonde

foxtail turned silver
disappear

The painful points
of thickets of leaves are finally dulled

Wild birds
little and fierce

sit singly on fence-wire
or hushed on the one slack power line

and distance sizzles like a damp firecracker
into the oncoming dark

For their help in completing this book, thanks are due to
Yaddo and Mr Curtis Harnack, to Michael Anania, to
James Ramholz, to Philip Levine, and to the many editors
kind enough to pre-publish poems from the sequence.

Some of the poems in this sequence appeared in earlier
versions and under different numbers in the following
magazines: *The American Poetry Review, The Christian Science
Monitor, The Iowa Review, Kayak, The Nation, New Letters, The
North American Review, Tri-Quarterly, The Black Warrior Review,
Poetry Now, The Mississippi Review,* and *The Hampden-Sydney
Poetry Review. The New Yorker* first published parts 3, 7 and 8
under the title 'The Woman on the Mall'; part 12 as 'The
Winter and the Snow'; part 35 as 'Vision and Transfor-
mation'; and part 36 as 'The Watergate Elegy.'

Other sections have been printed or reprinted in the
following anthologies: *Heartland* II and *Voyages to an Inland
Sea* III. Sections 29, 34 and 37 were printed as a broadside
by The Wine Press.

Of the original 59 sections of the sequence, seven have
been cut, three of which had been published previously
and are not listed here.